INCOME PRODUCING ASSETS

MAKING YOUR MONEY WORK FOR YOU

TABLE OF CONTENTS

Continuously Growing Your Passive Income

INTRODUCTION

Are you tired of the daily grind, trading your precious time for a paycheck that barely covers your bills and leaves you with little room for the life you truly desire? Have you dreamt of achieving financial freedom, where money works for you instead of the other way around? If so, then this book is the roadmap you've been searching for.

In this insightful and empowering book, we'll take you on a journey through the world of passive income, where financial independence is not just a distant dream but a tangible and achievable goal. We understand the common financial struggles that many people face, from living paycheck to paycheck to worrying about retirement savings, and we're here to help you break free from those constraints.

Chapter 1: Introduction to Passive Income

Our journey begins by introducing you to the concept of passive income and its pivotal role in achieving financial security and prosperity. We'll show you how shifting your mindset from active income (trading time for money) to passive income (money working for you) can open doors to endless possibilities.

Chapter 2: Building a Strong Financial Foundation

Before diving into the five income pillars, we'll equip you with the essential financial knowledge you need to succeed. Learn the art of budgeting, saving, and managing debt while building a robust financial foundation that will support your passive income journey.

Chapter 3: The First Pillar - Royalties

Discover the power of royalties as your first income pillar. Whether you're an author, musician, or inventor, we'll guide you through the process of earning money from your intellectual property. Learn how to turn your ideas and creations into consistent royalty streams that flow into your bank account.

Chapter 4: The Second Pillar - Rental Income

Real estate has long been a favored avenue for generating passive income. In this chapter, you'll explore the world of rental properties, from residential apartments to commercial spaces. We'll help you navigate property selection, management, and maintenance, ensuring that rental income becomes a reliable source of financial stability.

Chapter 5: The Third Pillar - Dividend Investing

Investing in dividend stocks can be a game-changer for your financial future. Discover how to build a diversified portfolio that generates regular dividend payments. We'll share strategies for selecting the right stocks, managing risk, and reinvesting dividends for exponential growth.

Chapter 6: The Fourth Pillar - Interest Income

Interest-bearing investments like savings accounts, certificates of deposit (CDs), and bonds provide a steady stream of income. Learn how to make the most of these low-risk options, optimizing your interest income while maintaining financial security.

Chapter 7: The Fifth Pillar - Capital Gains

Capital gains offer the potential for substantial wealth accumulation. Dive into investment strategies that capitalize on the power of capital appreciation. Whether you're a seasoned investor or a beginner, you'll gain insights into making smart investment choices and managing taxes on your gains.

Chapter 8: Diversification and Risk Management

As you build your passive income portfolio, it's crucial to understand the significance of diversification and risk management. This chapter offers valuable guidance on spreading your investments across different asset classes, minimizing risk, and achieving a balanced and resilient passive income strategy.

Chapter 9: Passive Income in Retirement

Retirement should be a time of relaxation and enjoyment, not financial worry. Discover how passive income can be your safety net during retirement. We'll explore various retirement income strategies, including tax-efficient withdrawal plans, so you can retire with confidence.

Chapter 10: Scaling Your Passive Income Streams

The journey doesn't end with a single income stream. In our final chapter, we'll show you how to scale up your passive income streams, so you can achieve financial abundance. Whether it's through entrepreneurship or expanding your investments, you'll learn how to keep your wealth growing.

Are you ready to take control of your financial destiny and break free from the limitations of traditional income sources? "INCOME PRODUCING ASSETS" is your definitive roadmap to financial freedom. With this book, you'll gain the knowledge, strategies, and confidence needed to embark on a life-changing journey toward financial independence.

Say goodbye to the stress of living paycheck to paycheck, worrying about retirement, or feeling trapped by your financial circumstances. Say hello to a world where your money works tirelessly for you, allowing you to live life on your terms. The benefits are clear: more time for family and hobbies, greater peace of mind, and the ability to pursue your dreams without financial constraints.

Don't let financial insecurity hold you back any longer. It's time to unlock your wealth potential and create a brighter future for yourself and your loved ones. Get started on your path to financial freedom with "INCOME PRODUCING ASSETS" today. Your journey to a prosperous and fulfilling life begins now.

Chapter 1: Introduction to Passive Income: The Road to Financial Freedom

Imagine waking up in the morning, not to the sound of a blaring alarm clock, but to the soft chirping of birds outside your window. You get out of bed when you're ready, not because you have to rush off to a job that you tolerate just to make ends meet. Your day is filled with activities you're passionate about, whether it's pursuing a hobby, spending quality time with loved ones, or even traveling the world. You're in control of your time and your life. This isn't a dream; it's the reality of financial freedom achieved through passive income.

Welcome to "INCOME PRODUCING ASSETS." In the following pages, we will explore the concept of passive income, its immense potential, and how you can harness it to transform your financial future. This isn't just another financial self-help book; it's a blueprint for achieving true financial independence.

Understanding the Concept of Passive Income

At its core, passive income represents earnings generated with minimal effort or active involvement. It's the money that flows into your bank account, even when you're not actively working. It's the opposite of the traditional 9-to-5 grind, where you trade your time for a fixed paycheck. Passive income empowers you to build wealth on your own terms.

To illustrate the concept, consider the following examples:

Royalties from Intellectual Property: Imagine you're a talented writer, and you've authored a bestselling novel. Every month, you receive royalty checks as readers around the world purchase your book. Whether you're writing new stories or sipping margaritas on a beach, the royalties keep rolling in.

Rental Income from Real Estate: You decide to invest in a rental property—a cozy apartment in a sought-after neighborhood. Each month, your tenants send you rent checks, covering not only your mortgage but also providing you with extra income. You don't have to fix leaky faucets or handle tenant complaints; you've hired a property manager to take care of those details.

Dividend Payments from Stocks: You've built a diversified portfolio of dividend-paying stocks. As a shareholder, you receive regular dividend payments from the companies you've invested in. These dividends provide a steady stream of income, whether you're actively monitoring the stock market or enjoying a leisurely weekend.

Interest from Investments: You've wisely parked your savings in a high-yield savings account and invested in bonds. These investments generate interest income, which gets credited to your account monthly. Your money is growing, and you don't need to constantly watch the markets.

Capital Gains from Investments: You're an astute investor who's carefully selected stocks and real estate properties. Over time, their values appreciate, and when you decide to sell them, you realize substantial capital gains. Your investment choices have turned into profitable assets.

Now, here's the exciting part: these examples represent just the tip of the iceberg. Passive income comes in various forms, each with its unique opportunities and potential. By understanding and strategically leveraging these income streams, you can create a diversified portfolio that not only covers your day-to-day expenses but also paves the way to financial abundance.

The Importance of Passive Income in Financial Freedom

Why is passive income so vital to achieving financial freedom? To answer that question, let's consider the common financial challenges that many people face:

The Rat Race: For most, the traditional model of trading time for money often leads to a never-ending cycle of work, paycheck, bills, and very little room for savings or enjoyment.

Limited Savings: With rising living costs, many struggle to save enough for emergencies, retirement, or financial goals beyond the basics.

Retirement Worries: The fear of not having enough money saved for retirement keeps people awake at night, causing anxiety and uncertainty about the future.

Life's Opportunities: Passions, hobbies, travel, and spending quality time with family often take a back seat to work and financial obligations.

Financial Insecurity: Economic downturns, job loss, and unexpected expenses can create financial crises that feel insurmountable.

This is where passive income steps in as a solution to these common problems:

Breaking Free from the 9-to-5: Passive income allows you to escape the daily grind, giving you the freedom to pursue what truly matters to you.

Building a Safety Net: With multiple passive income streams, you create a financial safety net that protects you from life's unexpected challenges.

Accelerating Wealth: Passive income isn't just about financial security; it's about accumulating wealth and creating a legacy for your loved ones.

Enhancing Quality of Life: Imagine having the time and resources to follow your passions, explore the world, and enjoy life's pleasures.

Creating Financial Peace: As your passive income grows, so does your peace of mind. The constant worry about bills and expenses diminishes, leaving you with a sense of tranquility.

But, as with any journey, the path to financial freedom through passive income requires careful planning, dedication, and knowledge. This book is your comprehensive guide, your trusted companion on this life-changing expedition.

Setting Financial Goals

Before we dive into the practical steps for building passive income streams, let's take a moment to talk about setting financial goals. Knowing what you want to achieve is the first step towards reaching your destination.

Consider the following questions:

What does financial freedom mean to you?

When do you want to achieve it?

What lifestyle changes or experiences do you aspire to have?

Do you have specific financial milestones in mind, such as buying a home, sending your kids to college, or retiring early?

Your answers to these questions will shape your financial journey and determine the strategies you'll employ. Whether you aim to quit your job, travel the world, or provide a secure future for your family, your goals will guide you every step of the way.

In the chapters that follow, we'll explore each of the five income pillars in detail, offering actionable insights, real-life examples, and expert tips to help you build and manage your passive income streams effectively. But remember, this journey is about more than just making money; it's about reclaiming your time, gaining control over your life, and achieving the financial freedom you've always dreamed of.

Are you ready to embark on this life-altering adventure? Let's get started on the path to unlocking your wealth through passive income.

In the upcoming chapters, we'll delve into the first income pillar - Royalties, and explore how it can transform your financial landscape.

Certainly! Here's Chapter 2, following the same guidelines and format:

Chapter 2: Building a Strong Financial Foundation

Picture this: You're building a magnificent skyscraper—one that will reach impressive heights. But before you start constructing the soaring towers, you need a solid foundation, one that can bear the weight and withstand the test of time. In the world of wealth-building, your financial foundation plays the same crucial role.

In this chapter, we'll lay the groundwork for your journey towards financial freedom by focusing on key principles:

Budgeting and Saving for Investment: Learn how to allocate your income effectively, create a budget that works for you, and save money that can be directed towards your passive income endeavors.

Managing Debt: Understand the impact of debt on your financial health and discover strategies for managing and reducing debt to accelerate your path to wealth.

Emergency Funds and Risk Management: Explore the importance of emergency funds and how risk management can safeguard your financial well-being.

Budgeting and Saving for Investment

Budgeting is like creating a treasure map for your financial journey—it shows you where your money comes from, where it goes, and how to make the most of every dollar. Let's dive in.

Understanding Your Cash Flow

To take control of your finances, you need to understand your cash flow. This means tracking your income and expenses meticulously. Consider using budgeting apps or software to streamline this process.

For example, if you earn $4,000 per month after taxes and your monthly expenses—including rent or mortgage, groceries, utilities, and transportation—total $3,500, you have $500 left over. This surplus is your financial breathing room, and it's where your passive income journey begins.

Creating a Budget that Works

A budget is your financial roadmap, guiding you toward your goals. It can be as simple as a spreadsheet or as high-tech as a dedicated app. Here's a basic breakdown of what your budget should include:

Income: List all sources of income, such as your salary, freelance work, or any other side hustles.

Fixed Expenses: These are regular, unchanging expenses like rent or mortgage, utilities, insurance, and loan payments.

Variable Expenses: These fluctuate from month to month, including groceries, dining out, entertainment, and discretionary spending.

Savings and Investments: Allocate a portion of your income to savings and investments, which will eventually become your passive income generators.

TIP: The 50/30/20 rule is a popular budgeting guideline. Allocate 50% of your income to needs (fixed expenses), 30% to wants (variable expenses), and 20% to savings and investments. Adjust these percentages to align with your goals.

Example: The 50/30/20 Budget

Let's consider the budget of an individual with a $4,000 monthly income:

Needs (50%): $2,000

Rent/Mortgage: $1,200

Utilities: $150

Transportation: $250

Insurance: $200

Loan Payments: $200

Wants (30%): $1,200

Groceries: $400

Dining Out: $200

Entertainment: $300

Discretionary Spending: $300

Savings and Investments (20%): $800

High-Yield Savings Account: $200

Retirement Account: $400

Passive Income Investments: $200

This budget ensures that essential needs are met, and a significant portion of income is directed towards savings and investments. Over time, the investments in the "Savings and Investments" category will become income-producing assets.

Managing Debt

Debt can be a heavy anchor that slows your progress towards financial freedom. While some types of debt, like a mortgage or student loans, may be considered acceptable and even beneficial, high-interest consumer debt can be crippling.

Prioritize High-Interest Debt

If you have high-interest debt, such as credit card balances, prioritize paying it down aggressively. The interest on these debts can accumulate rapidly and erode your financial stability. Consider strategies like the debt snowball (paying off the smallest balances first) or the debt avalanche (paying off the highest interest rate debts first) to tackle your debts effectively.

Build an Emergency Fund

Financial emergencies happen to everyone. Whether it's a medical bill, car repair, or unexpected job loss, having an emergency fund can provide a safety net when you need it most. Aim to save three to six months' worth of living expenses in an easily accessible account, like a high-yield savings account.

TIP: To jumpstart your emergency fund, allocate a portion of your tax refunds, bonuses, or any windfall money you receive directly to this fund.

Risk Management

Risk management is about protecting your financial well-being from unexpected events that could derail your progress. Here are some key aspects to consider:

Insurance: Review your insurance coverage, including health, auto, and home insurance. Ensure that you have adequate coverage to protect against unforeseen circumstances.

Estate Planning: Establish or update your will, power of attorney, and healthcare directives. This ensures that your assets are distributed according to your wishes and that your financial affairs are managed if you're unable to do so.

Investment Diversification: As you build your passive income portfolio, diversify your investments across different asset classes to spread risk. This will be explored in more detail in later chapters.

TIP: Periodically review your budget, debt reduction progress, and emergency fund status. Make adjustments as needed to stay on track with your financial goals.

In this chapter, we've laid the foundation for your journey to financial freedom through passive income. By mastering budgeting, managing debt effectively, and building a robust financial safety net, you're preparing yourself for the exciting adventure that lies ahead.

In Chapter 3, we'll dive into the first income pillar—Royalties. You'll learn how to turn your creative endeavors into a source of passive income that can transform your financial landscape. Stay tuned; your journey is just beginning.

Chapter 3: The First Pillar - Royalties

Imagine creating something truly exceptional—perhaps a novel, a piece of music, or an innovative invention. It's a masterpiece, a labor of love that you poured your heart and soul into. Now, picture this creation not only earning you recognition but also becoming a consistent source of income, flowing into your bank account month after month. This is the power of royalties—the first pillar of passive income.

In this chapter, we'll delve into the world of royalties, exploring what they are, how they work, and how you can turn your creative talents or intellectual property into a steady stream of income.

Exploring Royalties as a Passive Income Stream

At its core, royalties are payments made to the creator or owner of intellectual property for the use or distribution of that property. Intellectual property encompasses a wide range of creative works, including:

Books and Ebooks: Authors receive royalties from book sales.

Music: Musicians earn royalties when their songs are played on the radio, streamed online, or used in commercials.

Patents: Inventors receive royalties when other companies use their patented technology.

Art and Photography: Artists and photographers get royalties from the sale or licensing of their work.

Software: Developers collect royalties for the use of their software or apps.

The key to royalties as a passive income stream is that you create the work once, but it continues to generate income long after the initial effort.

Earning Royalties from Intellectual Property

Let's take a closer look at how royalties work for different types of intellectual property:

**1. Book Royalties:

If you're an author, your book can become a perpetual source of income. When your book is published, you'll typically receive a royalty percentage on each sale. The royalty rate varies depending on factors like the publisher, the format (print or digital), and your contract. For example, you might earn a 10% royalty on print book sales and a 30% royalty on ebook sales.

TIP: Self-publishing platforms like Amazon Kindle Direct Publishing (KDP) allow you to earn higher royalty rates, sometimes up to 70%, by selling ebooks directly to readers.

2. Music Royalties:

Musicians and songwriters can earn royalties in several ways, including:

Mechanical Royalties: Paid when your music is sold or streamed, typically through a record label or distributor.

Performance Royalties: Earned when your music is performed in public, whether on the radio, in a live concert, or on streaming platforms like Spotify.

Sync Licensing: Obtained when your music is used in commercials, movies, TV shows, or video games.

TIP: Join a performing rights organization like ASCAP, BMI, or SESAC to ensure you receive performance royalties whenever your music is played in public.

3. Patent Royalties:

If you've patented an innovative product or technology, other companies may want to use it. Licensing your patent allows these companies to use your invention in exchange for royalty payments. The amount of royalties can vary widely and is typically negotiated in licensing agreements.

TIP: Consulting with a patent attorney or intellectual property expert can help you negotiate favorable licensing terms and protect your intellectual property.

**4. Art and Photography Royalties:

Artists and photographers can earn royalties through the sale or licensing of their work. For example, photographers may license their photos to be used in advertisements, magazines, or websites, earning royalties each time the image is used.

TIP: Utilize online platforms like Shutterstock or Getty Images to reach a global audience and earn royalties from your photography.

Strategies for Maximizing Royalty Income

Earning royalties is not just about creating intellectual property; it's also about strategically managing and monetizing your creations. Here are some tips for maximizing your royalty income:

**1. Choose Your Medium Wisely:

Consider the type of intellectual property that aligns with your skills and interests. Are you a talented writer, musician, inventor, artist, or software developer? Focus on what you're passionate about, as this will drive your commitment and creativity.

**2. Market Your Work:

Creating great content or inventions is just the beginning. Effective marketing and promotion are essential for attracting an audience or potential users. Use social media, websites, and online communities to showcase your work.

**3. Leverage Online Platforms:

Take advantage of online platforms and marketplaces that allow you to reach a broader audience. For example, self-publishing platforms, music streaming services, and stock photography websites provide opportunities to earn royalties.

**4. Protect Your Intellectual Property:

Consider copyrighting your creative works or patenting your inventions to protect your rights and ensure you receive fair compensation.

**5. Negotiate Contracts Carefully:

If you work with publishers, record labels, or licensing partners, carefully review and negotiate contracts to secure favorable royalty terms.

Example: From Author to Royalty Earner

Let's follow the journey of Jane, a passionate writer who aspires to earn royalties from her novels:

Step 1: Write and Publish

Jane spends months crafting her debut novel. She chooses to self-publish through Amazon KDP, which offers higher royalty rates for ebooks.

Step 2: Market and Promote

Jane creates a website, builds an author platform on social media, and runs promotional campaigns to attract readers to her book.

Step 3: Earn Royalties

Her book gains traction, and readers purchase her ebook. With a 70% royalty rate on Kindle ebooks priced between $2.99 and $9.99, Jane earns $2.09 on each sale.

Step 4: Expand the Catalog

Jane continues to write and publish more novels, expanding her catalog and increasing her royalty income.

Step 5: Explore Other Avenues

She explores audiobook production and signs with a narrating talent for audiobook versions of her novels, further increasing her royalty income.

Conclusion

Royalties are a powerful and versatile source of passive income. Whether you're a creative writer, a musician, an inventor, an artist, or a software developer, your intellectual property has the potential to generate income long after the initial effort.

In Chapter 4, we'll dive into the second income pillar—Rental Income. You'll discover how real estate can become a reliable source of passive income and provide you with financial stability. Stay tuned; the journey continues.

Chapter 4: The Second Pillar - Rental Income

Imagine waking up on the first day of the month, opening your email, and seeing a series of notifications. They're not bills or reminders of financial obligations, but rent payments from your tenants. This is the magic of rental income—the second pillar of passive income.

In this chapter, we'll explore the world of rental properties, from residential apartments to commercial spaces. You'll learn how rental income works, the benefits it offers, and how to effectively manage your real estate investments.

Real Estate as an Income-Producing Asset

Real estate has long been regarded as one of the most reliable and effective ways to generate passive income. Unlike some forms of passive income that rely solely on intellectual property or financial markets, real estate investments are tangible, offering several advantages:

Steady Cash Flow: Rental properties typically provide a regular stream of rental income.

Appreciation: Over time, real estate properties can appreciate in value, potentially increasing your overall wealth.

Tax Benefits: Real estate investors often enjoy various tax advantages, including deductions for mortgage interest, property taxes, and depreciation.

Portfolio Diversification: Real estate can diversify your investment portfolio, reducing risk through asset allocation.

Types of Rental Properties

Rental income can be generated from various types of properties. Let's explore some of the most common:

1. Residential Properties:

Single-Family Homes: Owning single-family homes and renting them out is a straightforward way to start building rental income. You may choose to buy properties in desirable neighborhoods or areas with high rental demand.

Multi-Family Properties: Duplexes, triplexes, and apartment buildings allow you to earn rental income from multiple units within a single property.

2. Commercial Properties:

Office Spaces: Renting out office spaces to businesses and professionals can provide stable rental income.

Retail Spaces: Owning retail spaces in shopping centers or standalone locations allows you to earn rent from businesses.

Industrial Spaces: Warehouses, manufacturing facilities, and distribution centers can be lucrative rental properties for investors.

3. Vacation Rentals:

Short-Term Rentals: Renting out vacation homes or properties on platforms like Airbnb and VRBO can yield high rental income during peak tourist seasons.

TIP: The type of rental property you choose should align with your investment goals, budget, and risk tolerance.

Property Management and Passive Rental Income

While rental income can be an excellent source of passive income, it's essential to understand the level of involvement required to manage your properties effectively.

**1. Self-Management:

Pros: Maximum control over your properties, potentially saving money on property management fees.

Cons: Time-consuming, requires hands-on management, and can be stressful dealing with tenant issues and property maintenance.

**2. Property Management Services:

Pros: Professional property management companies handle day-to-day tasks, including tenant screening, maintenance, and rent collection.

Cons: Incurs management fees, which typically range from 8% to 12% of rental income.

**3. Hybrid Approach:

Pros: You can retain control over major decisions while outsourcing specific tasks, such as tenant screening or maintenance.

Cons: May require a more hands-on approach in certain areas.

Example: Residential Rental Property

Let's follow the journey of John, an investor who owns a residential rental property:

Step 1: Purchase Property

John purchases a single-family home in a suburban area known for its strong rental market. He secures financing through a mortgage.

Step 2: Tenant Screening

John carefully screens potential tenants, checking their credit history, rental references, and employment status. He selects a reliable tenant who signs a lease agreement.

Step 3: Rent Collection

Each month, John's tenant deposits the rent directly into his bank account. John ensures rent collection is hassle-free by using online payment methods.

Step 4: Property Maintenance

John maintains the property, addressing any repair or maintenance issues promptly. He also schedules routine inspections to keep the property in good condition.

Step 5: Passive Income Flow

Rental income flows into John's account regularly, covering the mortgage, property taxes, and maintenance costs. The surplus becomes his passive income.

Conclusion

Rental income is a powerful way to build passive income streams, providing financial stability and potentially allowing you to expand your real estate portfolio over time. However, effective property management and tenant relations are essential to ensure a smooth and profitable experience.

In Chapter 5, we'll explore the third income pillar—Dividend Investing. You'll discover how to select dividend stocks and build a portfolio that generates regular income, all while potentially benefiting from stock price appreciation. Stay tuned; your journey to financial freedom continues.

Chapter 5: The Third Pillar - Dividend Investing

Imagine owning a portfolio of stocks that not only grows in value over time but also pays you regularly, like a loyal friend handing you a dividend check. This is the beauty of dividend investing—the third pillar of passive income.

In this chapter, we'll dive into the world of dividend stocks, exploring how they work, the benefits they offer, and strategies for building a portfolio that generates a steady stream of income.

Understanding Dividend Stocks

Dividend stocks are shares of publicly traded companies that distribute a portion of their earnings to shareholders in the form of dividends. These dividends are typically paid on a regular basis, such as quarterly, and provide investors with a reliable source of income.

Let's explore the key components of dividend stocks:

**1. Dividend Yield:

The dividend yield is a crucial metric that tells you the annual dividend income as a percentage of the stock's price.

For example, if a stock is priced at $100 and pays an annual dividend of $4, its dividend yield is 4% ($4 divided by $100).

**2. Dividend History:

Reviewing a company's dividend history can provide insights into its commitment to paying dividends. Consistent dividend payments and a history of dividend growth are positive signs.

**3. Payout Ratio:

The payout ratio represents the percentage of a company's earnings paid out as dividends. A lower payout ratio suggests that the company has room to increase dividends in the future.

**4. Dividend Aristocrats:

Some companies have a long history of increasing their dividends year after year. These companies are often referred to as "Dividend Aristocrats" and are highly regarded by income investors.

Benefits of Dividend Investing

Dividend investing offers numerous advantages that make it an attractive option for those seeking passive income:

Regular Income: Dividend payments provide a predictable and regular stream of income, making it ideal for retirees or anyone looking to supplement their earnings.

Income Growth: Many dividend-paying companies increase their dividends over time, allowing you to benefit from rising income.

Stability: Dividend stocks often belong to established companies with stable cash flows, reducing the risk associated with some other types of investments.

Compound Growth: Reinvesting dividends by purchasing additional shares can accelerate the growth of your investment portfolio.

Building a Dividend Portfolio

To create a dividend portfolio that generates reliable income, you'll need to follow a structured approach:

**1. Selecting Dividend Stocks:

Focus on companies with a history of consistent dividend payments and dividend growth.

Consider diversifying across sectors to reduce risk.

Research a company's financial health, earnings stability, and future growth potential.

**2. Dividend Reinvestment:

Consider reinvesting your dividends to purchase additional shares of dividend-paying stocks. This strategy can lead to significant compound growth over time.

**3. Portfolio Diversification:

Diversify your dividend portfolio to reduce risk. Avoid concentrating too much in a single stock or sector.

Consider exchange-traded funds (ETFs) or mutual funds that focus on dividend-paying stocks for broader diversification.

**4. Monitor and Adjust:

Regularly review your dividend portfolio to ensure that the companies you've invested in continue to meet your criteria.

Adjust your portfolio as needed to maintain diversification and optimize your income.

Example: Building a Dividend Portfolio

Let's follow the journey of Sarah, an investor looking to build a dividend portfolio:

Step 1: Stock Selection

Sarah researches and selects a range of dividend-paying stocks from different sectors, including technology, healthcare, and consumer goods. She focuses on companies with a history of increasing dividends.

Step 2: Portfolio Diversification

To reduce risk, Sarah allocates her investments across various sectors. She avoids putting all her money into a single industry to maintain diversification.

Step 3: Dividend Reinvestment

Instead of taking cash dividends, Sarah opts to reinvest her dividends by using a dividend reinvestment plan (DRIP). This allows her to acquire additional shares without additional fees.

Step 4: Monitoring and Adjusting

Sarah periodically reviews her dividend portfolio, evaluating the performance of her stocks. If a company's dividend growth falters or if she identifies better opportunities, she adjusts her portfolio accordingly.

Conclusion

Dividend investing offers a straightforward path to passive income by building a portfolio of reliable dividend-paying stocks. As you accumulate shares and reinvest dividends, your income potential grows, bringing you closer to financial independence.

In Chapter 6, we'll explore the fourth income pillar—Interest Income. You'll discover how to make the most of interest-bearing investments, from high-yield savings accounts to bonds, and how to grow your interest income passively. Stay tuned; your journey towards financial freedom continues.

Chapter 6: The Fourth Pillar - Interest Income

Imagine your money working tirelessly in the background, silently growing while you go about your daily life. This is the power of interest income—the fourth pillar of passive income.

In this chapter, we'll explore the world of interest-bearing investments, from high-yield savings accounts to bonds. You'll learn how interest income works, the benefits it offers, and strategies for building a portfolio that generates a steady stream of passive income.

Understanding Interest Income

Interest income is earned by lending your money to financial institutions, governments, or corporations in exchange for periodic interest payments. It's a low-risk form of passive income that can be a valuable addition to your financial portfolio.

Let's dive into the key components of interest income:

1. Interest Rate:

The interest rate determines how much you'll earn on your investment. Higher interest rates typically yield greater income.

2. Principal Amount:

The initial amount you invest or deposit is known as the principal. Your interest income is calculated based on this amount.

3. Compounding:

Some interest-bearing investments offer compound interest, meaning that your interest earnings are reinvested, leading to exponential growth over time.

4. Maturity Date:

Bonds and other fixed-income investments often have a maturity date, at which point you'll receive your initial investment back along with any remaining interest.

Benefits of Interest Income

Interest income offers several advantages that make it an appealing choice for passive income:

Safety: Many interest-bearing investments, such as savings accounts and government bonds, are considered low-risk and provide a stable source of income.

Predictable Income: You can often count on regular interest payments, providing financial stability.

Liquidity: Some interest-bearing investments, like savings accounts and certificates of deposit (CDs), offer easy access to your funds when needed.

Diversification: Interest income can diversify your investment portfolio, reducing overall risk.

Types of Interest-Bearing Investments

There are various interest-bearing investment options to consider when building your passive income portfolio:

**1. High-Yield Savings Accounts:

High-yield savings accounts offer competitive interest rates, providing you with a safe and easily accessible way to earn interest on your cash.

**2. Certificates of Deposit (CDs):

CDs are time deposits with fixed terms and interest rates. They typically offer higher interest rates than regular savings accounts but require you to lock in your funds for a specific period.

**3. Government Bonds:

Government bonds are considered one of the safest investments. They include Treasury bills, notes, and bonds, each with different maturities and interest rates.

**4. Corporate Bonds:

Corporate bonds are issued by corporations to raise capital. They offer higher yields than government bonds but come with slightly higher risk.

**5. Municipal Bonds:

Municipal bonds are issued by state or local governments. They provide tax advantages for certain investors.

Building an Interest Income Portfolio

To create a portfolio that generates consistent interest income, you'll want to follow a systematic approach:

**1. Assess Your Risk Tolerance:

Consider your risk tolerance when selecting interest-bearing investments. Lower-risk options like high-yield savings accounts and government bonds are ideal for conservative investors.

**2. Diversify Your Holdings:

Diversification helps spread risk. Consider a mix of interest-bearing investments to balance safety and potential returns.

**3. Consider the Time Horizon:

Depending on your financial goals, you may choose short-term investments like high-yield savings accounts or longer-term options like bonds.

**4. Monitor and Reinvest:

Periodically review your interest income portfolio to ensure it aligns with your goals. Reinvest interest earnings to accelerate growth.

Example: Building an Interest Income Portfolio

Let's follow the journey of Mark, an investor looking to build an interest income portfolio:

Step 1: Assess Risk Tolerance

Mark assesses his risk tolerance and decides that he prefers lower-risk investments. He's willing to accept slightly lower returns in exchange for safety.

Step 2: Diversify Holdings

Mark allocates his funds across various interest-bearing investments, including a high-yield savings account, a CD ladder, and a mix of government bonds with varying maturities.

Step 3: Consider Time Horizon

Mark has both short-term and long-term financial goals. He keeps some funds in the high-yield savings account for liquidity and invests the rest in bonds with different maturity dates to match his goals.

Step 4: Monitor and Reinvest

Mark regularly checks the performance of his interest income portfolio. As his CDs mature, he reinvests the funds into new CDs to maintain a steady stream of interest income.

Conclusion

Interest income offers a reliable and low-risk way to build passive income. By strategically allocating your funds to interest-bearing investments, you can create a portfolio that provides financial stability and complements your other passive income streams.

In Chapter 7, we'll explore the fifth and final income pillar—Capital Gains. You'll discover how investing in assets like stocks and real estate can lead to significant wealth accumulation over time. Stay tuned; your journey towards financial freedom continues.

Chapter 7: The Fifth Pillar - Capital Gains

Imagine making an investment today and watching its value grow steadily over the years, eventually leading to substantial profits when you decide to sell. This is the essence of capital gains—the fifth and final pillar of passive income.

In this chapter, we'll delve into the world of capital gains, exploring how they work, the benefits they offer, and strategies for building a portfolio that accumulates wealth passively.

Understanding Capital Gains

Capital gains refer to the increase in the value of an asset, such as stocks, real estate, or other investments, over time. These gains are realized when you sell the asset at a higher price than what you initially paid.

Here are the key components of capital gains:

**1. Capital Appreciation:

Capital gains result from the appreciation of an asset's value. This can be driven by factors like market demand, economic conditions, and the asset's inherent qualities.

**2. Realized vs. Unrealized Gains:

Realized gains occur when you sell an asset, locking in the profit. Unrealized gains, on the other hand, represent the increase in value of an asset you still hold.

**3. Capital Gains Tax:

In many countries, capital gains are subject to taxation, but tax rates can vary based on factors like the holding period and your overall income.

Benefits of Capital Gains

Capital gains offer several advantages that make them an attractive pillar of passive income:

Wealth Accumulation: Over time, the growth of your investment portfolio can lead to significant wealth accumulation.

Flexibility: You have control over when you realize capital gains by choosing when to sell your assets.

Tax Efficiency: In some jurisdictions, long-term capital gains are taxed at a lower rate than regular income, providing tax advantages.

Diversification: Capital gains can be generated from a variety of assets, allowing you to diversify your investment portfolio.

Types of Capital Gains-Generating Investments

There are various types of investments that can generate capital gains:

**1. Stocks:

Investing in individual stocks or exchange-traded funds (ETFs) can lead to capital gains when the stock prices increase.

**2. Real Estate:

Real estate properties can appreciate in value over time, resulting in capital gains when you sell them.

**3. Collectibles and Art:

Rare collectibles, art, and antiques can appreciate significantly, creating capital gains for collectors.

**4. Business Ownership:

Owning a share of a business or a stake in a startup can result in capital gains if the business becomes more valuable.

Building a Capital Gains Portfolio

To create a portfolio that accumulates wealth through capital gains, you'll want to follow a strategic approach:

**1. Invest for the Long Term:

Capital gains are often more substantial when assets are held for an extended period. Consider a buy-and-hold strategy.

**2. Diversify Your Holdings:

Diversification can spread risk and increase the likelihood of realizing capital gains from various assets.

**3. Research and Analysis:

Conduct thorough research and analysis before making investment decisions. Understand the factors that can drive the appreciation of your chosen assets.

**4. Monitor and Adjust:

Regularly review your investment portfolio to ensure it aligns with your goals. Adjust your holdings as needed to optimize your potential for capital gains.

Example: Building a Capital Gains Portfolio

Let's follow the journey of Emily, an investor looking to build a portfolio that generates capital gains:

Step 1: Long-Term Focus

Emily adopts a long-term perspective for her investments. She plans to hold her assets for several years, allowing them to potentially appreciate in value significantly.

Step 2: Diversified Holdings

Emily diversifies her portfolio by investing in a mix of assets, including stocks, real estate, and collectibles. This diversification spreads her risk and increases her chances of realizing capital gains.

Step 3: Research and Analysis

Before making investment decisions, Emily conducts thorough research and analysis. For stocks, she assesses companies with strong growth potential. In real estate, she selects properties in areas with promising future development.

Step 4: Monitoring and Adjusting

Emily regularly reviews her investment portfolio to track the performance of her assets. If certain holdings show exceptional appreciation, she considers selling them to realize capital gains.

Conclusion

Capital gains provide a pathway to significant wealth accumulation through the appreciation of assets over time. By strategically building a portfolio that emphasizes long-term investments and diversification, you can harness the power of capital gains as the final pillar of your passive income strategy.

In the final chapter, we'll bring together the insights from all five income pillars to help you create a comprehensive passive income strategy that suits your financial goals. Stay tuned; your journey towards financial freedom is nearing its conclusion.

**1. Define Your Financial Objectives:

Start by setting clear financial goals. What do you hope to achieve with your passive income streams? Are you aiming for financial freedom, retirement income, or simply additional disposable income?

**2. Assess Your Risk Tolerance:

Understand your risk tolerance and comfort level with each passive income pillar. Some pillars, like high-yield savings accounts, offer lower risk but may yield lower returns, while others, like stocks, come with greater volatility and potential for higher rewards.

**3. Diversify Your Income Streams:

Diversification is key to reducing risk. Consider spreading your investments across multiple income pillars to create a well-rounded portfolio.

**4. Allocate Your Resources:

Determine how much capital you're willing to invest in each income pillar. Your allocation should align with your financial goals and risk tolerance.

**5. Create a Passive Income Timeline:

Develop a timeline for when you want to achieve specific passive income milestones. This can help guide your investment choices and strategies.

**6. Leverage the Power of Compound Growth:

Take advantage of compounding to accelerate the growth of your passive income. Reinvest dividends, interest, and capital gains to maximize your returns.

**7. Regularly Monitor and Adjust:

Stay engaged with your investments. Periodically review your portfolio's performance and make adjustments as needed to maintain alignment with your goals.

**8. Stay Informed and Educated:

The financial landscape evolves over time. Continuously educate yourself about new investment opportunities, strategies, and changes in tax laws that may affect your passive income.

**9. Seek Professional Advice:

If you're unsure about your investment decisions or need help navigating complex financial matters, consider consulting with a financial advisor or investment professional.

**10. Stay Committed and Patient:

Building a robust passive income portfolio takes time. Stay committed to your strategy and be patient, as long-term investments often yield the most substantial rewards.

Example: Crafting a Comprehensive Passive Income Strategy

Let's revisit the example of Sarah, who is looking to create a comprehensive passive income strategy:

Objective: Sarah's primary objective is to achieve financial independence and retire comfortably.

Risk Tolerance: Sarah has a moderate risk tolerance, comfortable with a mix of conservative and moderately aggressive investments.

Diversification: She allocates her resources across all five income pillars—Royalties (writing e-books), Rental Income (owning rental properties), Dividend Investing (stocks and ETFs), Interest Income (high-yield savings accounts and bonds), and Capital Gains (long-term stock investments).

Allocation: Sarah decides to allocate 40% of her capital to rental properties, 30% to dividend stocks, 15% to bonds and high-yield savings accounts, 10% to e-book royalties, and 5% to long-term stock investments.

Timeline: She sets a goal to achieve financial independence in 15 years, allowing her to retire at the age of 55.

Reinvestment: Sarah reinvests her dividends, interest income, and capital gains to harness the power of compounding.

Monitoring and Adjustment: Sarah reviews her portfolio annually, adjusting her allocation based on the performance of each income pillar.

Education: Sarah stays informed about changes in tax laws, investment opportunities, and market trends by regularly reading financial publications and attending seminars.

Chapter 8: Diversification and Risk Management

In your journey towards building a comprehensive passive income strategy, diversification and risk management play pivotal roles. These elements can help safeguard your investments and optimize your returns across the five income pillars—Royalties, Rental Income, Dividend Investing, Interest Income, and Capital Gains.

The Importance of Diversification

Diversification is a strategy that involves spreading your investments across different assets, asset classes, or income pillars. Its primary goal is to reduce risk by not putting all your financial eggs in one basket. Here's why diversification is essential:

**1. Risk Mitigation:

Different assets perform differently under various market conditions. By diversifying, you can reduce the impact of poor performance in any single investment or sector.

**2. Enhanced Returns:

Diversification can lead to more stable returns over time, as gains in one area may offset losses in another. This helps you achieve consistent growth.

**3. Liquidity:

Diversification can ensure that you have access to liquid assets even if some investments are less liquid. This is crucial for covering unexpected expenses.

Strategies for Balancing Risk and Return

While diversification is a cornerstone of risk management, it's essential to balance risk and return based on your financial goals and risk tolerance. Here are some strategies to consider:

**1. Asset Allocation:

Determine the optimal allocation of your resources among different income pillars. Consider your risk tolerance, time horizon, and financial objectives when making allocation decisions.

**2. Risk-Adjusted Returns:

Evaluate the risk-adjusted returns of your investments. Some assets may offer higher returns but come with increased volatility. Strike a balance that aligns with your comfort level.

**3. Rebalancing:

Regularly review your portfolio and adjust your allocation if it deviates significantly from your target. Rebalancing ensures that your risk remains in check.

**4. Stress Testing:

Conduct stress tests on your portfolio to assess how it may perform under adverse market conditions. This can help you prepare for potential downturns.

Asset Allocation in Passive Income Portfolios

Asset allocation involves determining the mix of assets within each income pillar to optimize your passive income portfolio. Here's how asset allocation applies to each income pillar:

**1. Royalties:

Diversify your royalties by creating a mix of different types of intellectual property, such as books, music, and patents. Consider varying your creative endeavors to minimize reliance on one source.

**2. Rental Income:

In the real estate sector, diversify by owning properties in different locations and property types (e.g., residential and commercial). This can help mitigate the impact of regional economic fluctuations.

**3. Dividend Investing:

Diversify your dividend stocks by selecting companies from various sectors, industries, and regions. Consider dividend-focused ETFs for broad diversification.

**4. Interest Income:

Diversify your interest income by allocating funds to different interest-bearing investments, such as high-yield savings accounts, bonds with varying maturities, and peer-to-peer lending platforms.

**5. Capital Gains:

Diversify your capital gains investments by holding a mix of asset classes, including stocks, real estate, and collectibles. This can help spread risk across different growth opportunities.

Conclusion

Diversification and risk management are fundamental to building a resilient and successful passive income strategy. By carefully considering asset allocation, balancing risk and return, and regularly reviewing your portfolio, you can optimize your chances of achieving your financial goals while safeguarding your investments.

In Chapter 9, we'll explore how passive income can be a key component of your retirement plan. You'll learn strategies for achieving financial independence through passive income streams and creating a secure financial future in your retirement years. Stay tuned; your journey towards financial freedom continues.

Chapter 9: Passive Income in Retirement

As you plan for retirement, passive income can be a crucial component of your financial strategy. In this chapter, we'll explore how passive income streams can provide you with the financial independence and security you desire during your retirement years.

Achieving Financial Independence through Passive Income

Retirement marks a significant life transition, and achieving financial independence is a primary goal. Passive income can play a pivotal role in making your retirement dreams a reality. Here's how:

**1. Financial Freedom:

Passive income sources can supplement your retirement savings, reducing your reliance on a fixed retirement nest egg.

**2. Stress Reduction:

A well-structured passive income strategy can alleviate financial stress during retirement, allowing you to focus on enjoying your life.

**3. Flexibility:

Passive income provides flexibility in your retirement lifestyle. You can choose to travel, pursue hobbies, or spend quality time with loved ones without worrying about finances.

Retirement Income Planning

To effectively incorporate passive income into your retirement plan, consider these strategies:

1. Determine Your Retirement Income Needs:

Calculate your expected retirement expenses, including housing, healthcare, travel, and entertainment. This will help you establish a baseline for your passive income requirements.

2. Assess Your Current Passive Income Streams:

Evaluate your existing passive income sources, such as investments, royalties, and rental income. Determine how they align with your retirement income needs.

3. Maximize Social Security Benefits:

Understand the Social Security benefits available to you and determine the optimal age to start receiving them based on your circumstances.

4. Create a Diverse Passive Income Portfolio:

Diversify your passive income sources to spread risk. A mix of investments, rental properties, royalties, and more can help ensure a steady income flow.

**5. Consider Longevity:

Plan for a retirement that could last several decades. Ensure that your passive income strategy can sustain you through your entire retirement.

Tax-Efficient Withdrawal Strategies

Managing taxes is essential during retirement to preserve your passive income. Consider these tax-efficient withdrawal strategies:

**1. Tax-Deferred Accounts:

Withdraw funds from tax-deferred accounts like IRAs and 401(k)s strategically to minimize tax liabilities.

**2. Roth Accounts:

Roth IRAs and Roth 401(k)s offer tax-free withdrawals in retirement. Consider converting traditional retirement accounts into Roth accounts if it aligns with your tax strategy.

**3. Capital Gains:

Capital gains from investments held for over a year may qualify for lower tax rates. Plan your investment sales to optimize capital gains taxes.

**4. Required Minimum Distributions (RMDs):

Be aware of RMD rules for retirement accounts to avoid penalties. Plan your withdrawals accordingly to meet RMD requirements.

Conclusion

Passive income is not just a path to financial freedom; it's also a crucial element of a secure and fulfilling retirement. By planning ahead, diversifying your passive income streams, and implementing tax-efficient strategies, you can enjoy the retirement lifestyle you've always envisioned.

In Chapter 10, we'll explore how to scale your passive income streams to reach new levels of financial success. Whether you're looking to expand your existing income sources or explore entrepreneurial opportunities, you'll find valuable insights on scaling your passive income. Stay tuned; your journey towards financial freedom continues.

Chapter 10: Scaling Your Passive Income Streams

As you progress on your journey toward financial freedom, you may reach a point where you're ready to take your passive income to the next level. In this chapter, we'll explore strategies for scaling your passive income streams, allowing you to achieve even greater financial success.

Scaling Up Your Income Streams

Scaling your passive income streams involves increasing the size, scope, or efficiency of your existing sources of income. Here are some effective strategies to scale up:

**1. Expand Your Investments:

Consider increasing your investments in assets like stocks, real estate, or businesses to generate higher returns. This could involve purchasing additional shares, acquiring more rental properties, or investing in growth stocks.

**2. Leverage Technology:

Embrace technology to enhance the efficiency of your passive income activities. For example, automate your online business operations or use robo-advisors for investment management.

**3. Explore New Income Avenues:

Look for additional passive income opportunities within your existing income pillars. For instance, if you have successful e-books generating royalties, consider writing more books or exploring audiobook production.

**4. Diversify Your Portfolio:

Explore new income pillars or asset classes to diversify your portfolio further. This could involve branching into different types of real estate, investing in dividend-paying stocks from various sectors, or exploring alternative investments like peer-to-peer lending.

Entrepreneurship and Passive Income

Another way to scale your passive income is through entrepreneurship. Here's how entrepreneurship and passive income can intersect:

**1. Create Online Businesses:

Launch online ventures like e-commerce stores, blogs, or niche websites that can generate passive income through advertising, affiliate marketing, or product sales.

**2. Build and Sell Digital Products:

Create digital products such as online courses, software, or digital downloads that provide recurring income when customers purchase or subscribe.

**3. Outsource and Delegate:

As your online businesses grow, consider outsourcing tasks to freelancers or hiring virtual assistants to manage day-to-day operations, allowing you to focus on strategic growth.

**4. Invest in Passive Business Ventures:

Explore opportunities to invest in businesses as a silent partner or through crowdfunding platforms. This can provide you with a share of the business's profits without active involvement.

Continuously Growing Your Passive Income

Scaling your passive income is an ongoing process. To ensure sustainable growth, follow these principles:

**1. Set Clear Goals:

Define specific financial goals for scaling your passive income streams. Having a target will keep you motivated and focused.

**2. Regularly Review Your Portfolio:

Periodically assess the performance of your investments and income sources. Make adjustments as needed to optimize returns.

**3. Stay Informed:

Continuously educate yourself about new investment opportunities, market trends, and emerging passive income strategies.

**4. Reinvest Your Earnings:

Consider reinvesting a portion of your passive income earnings into new income-producing ventures or assets to fuel further growth.

Conclusion

Scaling your passive income streams can propel you towards financial freedom and open doors to exciting opportunities. Whether you're expanding your existing income sources, exploring entrepreneurial endeavors, or diversifying your portfolio, the possibilities for growth are limitless.

Your journey towards financial independence and security is a dynamic one. Stay committed, remain adaptable, and keep exploring new avenues for passive income. With perseverance and strategic planning, you can reach new heights of financial success. Congratulations on embarking on this transformative journey!

Bonus Chapter: Exploring Additional Passive Income Opportunities

In addition to the five core passive income pillars we've explored, there are several other avenues you can consider to diversify and expand your passive income portfolio. In this bonus chapter, we'll delve into these additional passive income opportunities, each offering its own unique potential for generating income.

Peer-to-Peer Lending

Peer-to-peer (P2P) lending platforms have gained popularity as an alternative investment. Here's how it works:

**1. Lender Role:

As a lender, you provide loans to individuals or small businesses through online platforms.

In return, you receive interest payments on the principal amount loaned.

**2. Risk and Returns:

P2P lending offers higher potential returns compared to traditional savings accounts, but it comes with varying levels of risk depending on borrower creditworthiness.

Stock Options Trading

Stock options provide an opportunity to profit from the price movements of individual stocks or indices. Here's how stock options trading can generate passive income:

**1. Selling Covered Calls:

If you own shares of a stock, you can sell covered call options against those shares.

You receive premiums from selling these options, providing a source of income.

2. Cash-Secured Puts:

You can also sell cash-secured put options, committing to buying shares at a predetermined price if the option is exercised.

If the put option expires unexercised, you keep the premium.

Forex Trading

Foreign exchange (Forex) trading involves the exchange of one currency for another. While it carries higher risks, it can be a source of passive income through the following methods:

1. Carry Trade:

Involves borrowing funds in a currency with a low-interest rate and investing in a currency with a higher interest rate.

The interest rate differential generates passive income.

**2. Algorithmic Trading:

Utilizing automated trading systems or algorithms to execute trades based on predefined criteria.

Requires technical expertise and careful strategy development.

Tax Liens and Deeds

Investing in tax liens and tax deeds can be a unique way to generate passive income through real estate. Here's how it works:

**1. Tax Liens:

When property owners fail to pay property taxes, local governments may auction off tax liens to investors.

Investors purchase these liens and earn interest when property owners redeem them by paying the overdue taxes.

**2. Tax Deeds:

In some cases, if property owners do not redeem the tax lien within a specified period, investors may acquire the property through a tax deed auction.

Conclusion

While the five core passive income pillars provide a solid foundation, there are numerous additional opportunities to explore. Peer-to-peer lending, stock options trading, Forex trading, tax liens, and deeds are just a few examples of the diverse options available.

As you consider these opportunities, it's essential to conduct thorough research, understand the associated risks, and develop a strategy that aligns with your financial goals and risk tolerance. Diversifying your passive income sources can enhance your financial stability and bring you one step closer to achieving true financial freedom.

Remember that passive income success often requires a combination of dedication, continuous learning, and adaptability. By exploring and leveraging these additional opportunities, you can create a well-rounded passive income portfolio that works for you. Best of luck on your journey to financial independence!

CONCLUSION

Conclusion: Your Path to Financial Freedom

Congratulations on completing your journey through the world of passive income and exploring the various income pillars, strategies, and opportunities that can lead you to financial freedom. In this conclusion, we'll revisit the key takeaways, summarize the core principles of passive income, and offer some final words of guidance to empower you on your path to financial success.

Reflecting on Your Journey

Over the course of this book, we've embarked on a comprehensive exploration of passive income—what it is, how it works, and how you can harness its power to achieve your financial goals. We've delved into the five core passive income pillars:

Royalties: Creating and licensing intellectual property like books, music, and patents to earn ongoing royalties.

Rental Income: Owning and renting out real estate properties, whether residential or commercial, to generate a consistent stream of income.

Dividend Investing: Investing in dividend-paying stocks and exchange-traded funds (ETFs) to earn regular dividend payments.

Interest Income: Lending your money to financial institutions, governments, or corporations in exchange for periodic interest payments.

Capital Gains: Accumulating wealth through the appreciation of assets like stocks, real estate, and collectibles.

Each of these income pillars offers unique advantages and opportunities, and you've learned how to strategically build and diversify your passive income portfolio by combining them to create a resilient and robust source of wealth.

The Comprehensive Passive Income Strategy

As you've discovered, crafting a comprehensive passive income strategy involves a series of steps and considerations. Here's a recap of the core principles that have guided you throughout this journey:

Define Your Financial Objectives: Set clear and specific financial goals that passive income can help you achieve, whether it's financial freedom, retirement income, or additional disposable income.

Assess Your Risk Tolerance: Understand your comfort level with risk and align your passive income strategy with your risk tolerance.

Diversify Your Income Streams: Spread your investments and income sources across various pillars and asset classes to reduce risk and enhance stability.

Allocate Your Resources: Determine how much capital you're willing to invest in each income pillar based on your financial goals and risk tolerance.

Create a Passive Income Timeline: Develop a timeline for when you want to achieve specific passive income milestones, helping guide your investment choices.

Leverage Compound Growth: Take advantage of the power of compounding by reinvesting dividends, interest, and capital gains to maximize returns.

Regularly Monitor and Adjust: Stay engaged with your investments, periodically reviewing your portfolio's performance, and making adjustments to maintain alignment with your goals.

Stay Informed and Educated: Continuously educate yourself about new investment opportunities, strategies, and changes in tax laws that may affect your passive income.

Seek Professional Advice: When necessary, consult with a financial advisor or investment professional to navigate complex financial matters.

Stay Committed and Patient: Building a robust passive income portfolio takes time. Stay committed to your strategy and be patient, as long-term investments often yield the most substantial rewards.

Passive Income in Retirement

In Chapter 9, we explored how passive income can play a pivotal role in your retirement plan. Achieving financial independence during retirement is a common goal, and passive income can help you realize this dream. We covered essential strategies, including:

Determining Your Retirement Income Needs: Calculate your expected retirement expenses to establish a baseline for your passive income requirements.

Assessing Your Current Passive Income Streams: Evaluate your existing passive income sources and how they align with your retirement income needs.

Maximizing Social Security Benefits: Understand Social Security benefits and determine the optimal age to start receiving them based on your circumstances.

Creating a Diverse Passive Income Portfolio: Diversify your passive income sources to ensure a steady income flow throughout retirement.

Tax-Efficient Withdrawal Strategies: Implement tax-efficient strategies to manage taxes and preserve your passive income.

Scaling Your Passive Income Streams

Chapter 10 introduced the concept of scaling your passive income, taking your financial journey to new heights. We explored strategies for:

Scaling Up Your Income Streams: Increasing the size, scope, or efficiency of your existing income sources, including expanding investments and leveraging technology.

Entrepreneurship and Passive Income: Venturing into entrepreneurship to create additional passive income streams, such as online businesses, digital product creation, and passive investments.

Continuously Growing Your Passive Income: Setting clear goals, regularly reviewing your portfolio, staying informed, and reinvesting your earnings to achieve ongoing growth.

Exploring Additional Passive Income Opportunities

In the bonus chapter, we explored various additional passive income opportunities that can complement your existing income pillars. These opportunities include:

Peer-to-Peer Lending: Earning interest by providing loans to individuals or small businesses through online platforms.

Stock Options Trading: Generating income through strategies like selling covered calls and cash-secured puts in the stock market.

Forex Trading: Exploring currency trading for passive income, including carry trades and algorithmic trading.

Tax Liens and Deeds: Investing in tax liens and tax deeds as an alternative real estate investment strategy.

Embracing the Journey

Your journey towards financial freedom is a dynamic process filled with opportunities, challenges, and learning experiences. As you reflect on your path, remember these essential principles:

Patience: Building wealth through passive income takes time. Stay committed to your long-term goals, and don't be discouraged by short-term fluctuations.

Education: Continue to educate yourself about investment strategies, financial markets, and emerging opportunities. Knowledge is a powerful tool on your journey.

Adaptability: Be prepared to adapt your passive income strategy as circumstances change. Flexibility is key to staying on course.

Risk Management: Always consider risk when making investment decisions. Diversification and careful planning can help mitigate potential losses.

Enjoy the Journey: Ultimately, the goal of financial freedom is to enhance your quality of life. Don't forget to enjoy the fruits of your labor along the way.

Give Back: As you achieve financial success, consider giving back to your community or supporting causes that matter to you. Making a positive impact can be a fulfilling part of your journey.

Final Thoughts

Your journey towards financial freedom through passive income is an empowering and transformative endeavor. By understanding the principles, strategies, and opportunities presented in this book, you've laid a solid foundation for building a secure and prosperous financial future.

Remember that the path to financial freedom is unique for each individual. Tailor your passive income strategy to your goals, preferences, and circumstances. Stay focused, stay motivated, and stay the course. Whether you're aiming for early retirement, funding your dream lifestyle, or securing a comfortable retirement, the possibilities are within your reach.

As you embark on your journey, know that you have the knowledge and tools to navigate the world of passive income successfully. The future is filled with potential, and with dedication and strategic planning, you can achieve the financial freedom and security you desire.

Thank you for joining us on this enlightening and transformative journey. Your financial freedom begins now.